Bond

Verbal Reasoning
Assessment Papers

8–9 years

J M Bond

Nelson Thornes

First published in 2002 by:
Nelson Thornes Ltd

This edition published in 2007 by:
Nelson Thornes Ltd
Delta Place
27 Bath Road
CHELTENHAM
GL53 7TH
United Kingdom

11 12 / 10 9 8

A catalogue record for this book is available from the British Library

ISBN 978 0 7487 8110 2

Page make-up by Tech Set Ltd

Printed and bound in Egypt by Sahara Printing Company

Before you get started

What is Bond?

This book is part of the Bond Assessment Papers series for verbal reasoning, which provides a **thorough and continuous course in verbal reasoning** from ages six to twelve. It builds up verbal reasoning skills from book to book over the course of the series.

What does this book cover?

Verbal reasoning questions can be grouped into four distinct groups: sorting words, selecting words, anagrams, coded sequences and logic. This book practises a wide range of questions appropriate to the age group drawn from all these categories. One of the key features of Bond Assessment Papers is that each one practises **a very wide variety of skills and question types** so that children are always challenged to think – and don't get bored repeating the same question type again and again. We believe that variety is the key to effective learning. It helps children 'think on their feet' and cope with the unexpected.

The age given on the cover is for guidance only. As the papers are designed to be reasonably challenging for the age group, any one child may naturally find him or herself working above or below the stated age. The important thing is that children are always encouraged by their performance. Working at the right level is the key to this.

What does the book contain?

- **20 papers** – each one contains 45 questions.
- **Scoring devices** – there are score boxes next to the questions and a Progress Chart at the back. The chart is a visual and motivating way for children to see how they are doing. Encouraging them to colour in the chart as they go along and to try to beat their last score can be highly effective!
- **Next Steps** – advice on what to do after finishing the papers can be found on the inside back cover.
- **Answers** – located in an easily-removed central pull-out section. If you lose your answers, please email cservices@nelsonthornes.com for another copy.

How can you use this book?

One of the great strengths of Bond Assessment Papers is their flexibility. They can be used at home, school and by tutors to:

- provide regular verbal reasoning practice in **bite-sized chunks**
- **highlight strengths and weaknesses** in the core skills
- identify **individual needs**
- set **homework**
- set **timed formal practice tests** – allow about 30 minutes.

It is best to start at the beginning and work through the papers in order.

What does a score mean and how can it be improved?

If children colour in the Progress Chart at the back, this will give an idea of how they are doing. The Next Steps inside the back cover will help you to decide what to do next to help a child progress. We suggest that it is always valuable to go over any wrong answers with children.

Don't forget the website...!

Visit www.bond11plus.co.uk for lots of advice, information and suggestions on everything to do with Bond, helping children to do their best, and exams.

Paper 1

Underline the pair of words most similar in meaning.

Example   come, go   <u>roam, wander</u>   fear, fare

1 alley, lane   real, false   back, forward

2 good, bad   bake, oven   heavy, weighty

3 beat, lose   bite, nip   bath, room

4 nose, face   shallow, river   correct, right

5 come, go   sorry, glad   closed, shut

5

Find the three-letter word which can be added to the letters in capitals to make a new word. The new word will complete the sentence sensibly.

Example   The cat sprang onto the MO.   <u>USE</u>

6 SN days make a week.   _____

7 We put SS on our feet.   _____

8 He FED his cup.   _____

9 They SED me the way to the town.   _____

10 I would like to hear a story BEE I go to sleep.   _____

5

Underline two words, one from each group, that go together to form a new word. The word in the first group always comes first.

Example   (hand, <u>green</u>, for)   (light, <u>house</u>, sure)

11 (is, be, it)   (bed, low, high)

12 (shut, open, in)   (side, back, air)

13 (for, form, fear)   (car, got, back)

14 (toe, finger, hand)   (rip, tip, side)

15 (face, hair, hand)   (shave, some, were)

5

Change the first word of the third pair in the same way as the other pairs to give a new word.

Example   bind, hind   bare, hare   but, <u>hut</u>

16   art, part   ale, pale   ant,   _____

17   ill, till   all, tall   ear,   _____

18   pick, prick   feed, freed   tied,   _____

19   ran, rain   man, main   pan   _____

20   top, stop   tar, star   tab,   _____

5

Fill in the missing letters. The alphabet has been written out to help you.

A B C D E F G H I J K L M N O P Q R S T U V W X Y Z

Example   A B is to C D as P Q is to <u>R S</u>

21   A is to D as G is to   ____

22   3B is to 4D as 5F is to   ____

23   ABD is to BCE as CDF is to ____

24   MAB is to NBC as OCD is to ____

25   9AB is to 8CD as 7EF is to   ____

5

Fill in the crosswords so that all the given words are included. You have been given one letter as a clue in each crossword.

26

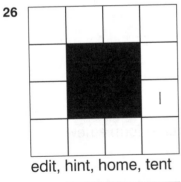

edit, hint, home, tent

27

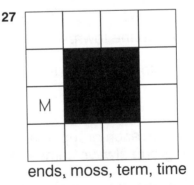

ends, moss, term, time

28

heap, ship, wags, wish

3

Fill in the missing number in each sequence.

Example   2   4   6   8   <u>10</u>

29 12   15   _____   21   24

30 1996   1998   _____   2002   2004

31 20   17   14   11   _____

32 4.5   5.0   5.5   6.0   _____

33 17   _____   23   26   29

34 20   18   15   11   _____

6

If the code for PEARS is 13579, what are the codes for the following words?

35 ARE _____   **36** RAP _____

37 SPA _____   **38** SEE _____

39 PEA _____

What do these codes stands for?

40 91357 _____   **41** 511357 _____

7

Here are some TV programmes.

> 14:00 Play School
>
> 14:15 Cartoons
>
> 15:30 Think Twice
>
> 16:00 The School on the Hill
>
> 16:30 News

How many minutes do these programmes last?

42 Play School ___ minutes   **43** Cartoons ___ minutes

44 Think Twice ___ minutes   **45** The School on the Hill ___ minutes

4

Underline the word in brackets closest in meaning to the word in capitals.

Example   UNHAPPY (unkind death laughter <u>sad</u> friendly)

1 CLEVER   (school bright pupil stupid trick)

2 QUICK   (slow fast speed walk step)

3 LAUGH   (cry taught funny chuckle humour)

4 MODERN   (easy today young new trend)

5 SIMPLE   (crazy silly hard easy straight)

5

Complete the following sentences in the best way by choosing one word from each set of brackets.

Example   Tall is to (tree, <u>short</u>, colour) as narrow is to
(thin, white, <u>wide</u>).

6 Top is to (bottom, pot, over) as fat is to (side, thin, chubby).

7 Fair is to (fear, dark, shop) as clean is to (wash, dirty, soap).

8 Short is to (fat, thin, tall) as lost is to (win, one, found).

9 Full is to (empty, over, cup) as rough is to (tumble, cross, smooth).

10 Shut is to (open, close, key) as fast is to (slow, speed, late).

5

Find the letter which will end the first word and start the second word.

Example   peac (<u>h</u>) ome

11 han (—) oor

12 mat (—) ver

13 sal (—) ill

14 duc (—) ite

15 mas (—) est

5

Fill in the crosswords so that all the given words are included. You have been given one letter as a clue in each crossword.

16

cats, camp, plum, sham

17

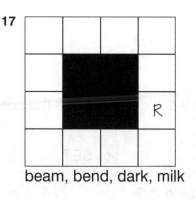

beam, bend, dark, milk

18

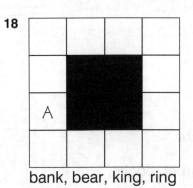

bank, bear, king, ring

Underline two words, one from each group, that go together to form a new word. The word in the first group always comes first.

Example (hand, <u>green</u>, for)   (light, <u>house</u>, sure)

19 (bed, for, right)   (tub, cot, side)

20 (near, after, under)   (some, ground, set)

21 (in, an, it)   (left, form, just)

22 (far, near, out)   (law, police, here)

23 (far, for, ran)   (take, give, us)

5

3

Change the first word into the last word by changing one letter at a time and making a new word in the middle.

Example   CASE *CASH* LASH

24 PANE _____   PINK

25 COMB _____   HOME

5

26 HOPE _____ COPY

27 HATE _____ MITE

28 COLD _____ GILD

5

If the code for POSTER is 235689, what are the codes for the following words?

29 STOP _____   30 SET _____

What do these codes stand for?

31 632 _____   32 6355 _____

33 899 _____

5

Choose the word or phrase that makes each sentence true.

Example A LIBRARY always has (posters, a carpet, <u>books</u>, DVDs, stairs).

34 A HOUSE always has (a garage, curtains, walls, a doorbell, a fence).

35 A LAKE always has (ducks, boats, fish, swans, water).

36 A CITY always has (farms, buildings, an airport, an underground, a river).

37 A KITCHEN always has (a table, chairs, a stove, plants, a radio).

38 A SCHOOL always has (a cafeteria, a nurse, students, a swimming pool, a bus).

5

Underline the two words which are made from the same letters.

Example TAP PET <u>TEA</u> POT <u>EAT</u>

39 MEAT TIME TUNE TEAM MUST

40 NUT TEN NET TAN NOT

41 TEST STAB LAST LOST SALT

3

Remove one letter from the word in capitals to leave a new word.
The meaning of the new word is given in the clue.

Example   A U N T   an insect   _ant_

42 FARM   not near   _____

43 HARM   a piece of meat   _____

44 GROUND   shaped like a ball   _____

45 THAN   you get it from sunbathing _____   4

Now go to the Progress Chart to record your score!   Total   45

Paper 3

Underline the two words which are the odd ones out in the following groups
of words.

Example   black   king   purple   green   house

1 noisy   peaceful   crowd   calm   concert

2 small   short   enlarge   brief   expand

3 sea   harbour   ocean   pier   lake

4 sturdy   weak   strong   healthy   ill

5 walk   swim   stride   dive   march   5

Find the three-letter word which can be added to the letters in capitals to
make a new word. The new word will complete the sentence sensibly.

Example   The cat sprang onto the MO.   USE

6 The weather was W and sunny.   _____

7 He SCHED high and low for the remote control. _____

8 I've got some nice, new PYAS to wear.   _____

9 My favourite fruit is an APRI.   _____

10 The octopus got him with its TACLES.   _____   5

7

Which one letter can be added to the front of all of these words to make new words?

Example   _c_are   _c_at   _c_rate   _c_all

11 ___late   ___lease   ___ony   ___each

12 ___right   ___ig   ___all   ___ean

13 ___how   ___et   ___poon   ___nake

14 ___elt   ___eal   ___at   ___oan

15 ___hall   ___eal   ___mall   ___nail

5

Add one letter to the word in capital letters to make a new word. The meaning of the new word is given in the clue.

Example   PLAN   simple   _plain_

16 TROT   a fish   _____

17 NOSE   the opposite of silence   _____

18 TICK   the opposite of thin   _____

19 LATE   used to put our food on   _____

20 SORT   different types of games   _____

5

Fill in the crosswords so that all the given words are included. You have been given one letter as a clue in each crossword.

21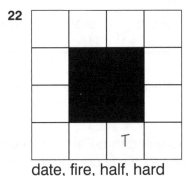

keep, mark, mist, trip

22

date, fire, half, hard

23

part, pear, ripe, tide

3

Fill in the missing number in each sequence.

Example 2 4 6 8 *10*

24 3   6   9   —   15

25 12   10   8   —   4

26 12   24   —   48   60

27 21   32   43   —   65

28 121   232   —   454   565

○ 5

These words have been written in code, but the codes are not under the right words.

TOO   OUT   TOT   TO   UP

72   722   247   46   727

Write the correct code for each word.

29 TOO _____   30 OUT _____

31 TOT _____   32 TO _____

33 UP _____

○ 5

If a = 1, b = 2, c = 3, find the sum of:

34 a + b + c = _____   35 c + 2b = _____

36 2a + 2b = _____

○ 3

Underline the one word which **cannot be made** from the letters of the word in capital letters.

Example S T A T I O N E R Y stones tyres ration <u>nation</u> noisy

37 CONSIDER   cried   nice   dear   rice   coin

38 LOWEST   low   west   flow   sew   owl

39 TEACHER   eaten   chat   ear   are   crate

40 INSIDE   den   snide   end   dine   need

○ 4

In each line, underline the word which has its letters in alphabetical order.

41 gas   guzzle   grunt   got

42 apple   ant   ask   ale

43 clever   caution   care   cry

44 deal   dint   dream   drink

45 flow   flea   frank   frog

Now go to the Progress Chart to record your score!   Total   5

45

Paper 4

Find and underline the two words which need to change places for each sentence to make sense.

Example She went to <u>letter</u> the <u>write</u>.

1 The tail wagged her dog when she saw the treat.

2 My sister told my mother to finish her homework.

3 I like to read a bed before book.

4 At my birthday cake we ate ice cream and party.

5 My mum takes the office to her bus.

5

Underline two words, one from each group, that go together to form a new word. The word in the first group always comes first.

Example (hand, <u>green</u>, for)   (light, <u>house</u>, sure)

6 (wood, light, sea)   (day, tree, weed)

7 (earth, glass, sand)   (sun, castle, rain)

8 (well, work, pail)   (shop, cut, know)

9 (foot, glove, hand)   (knee, head, shake)

10 (under, over, through)   (sky, place, water)

5

Fill in the crosswords so that all the given words are included. You have been given one letter as a clue in each crossword.

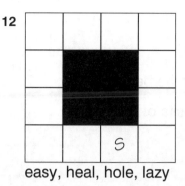

11

12

keen, park, port, torn

easy, heal, hole, lazy

2

Underline one word in the brackets which is most opposite in meaning to the word in capitals.

Example WIDE (broad   vague   long   <u>narrow</u>   motorway)

13 HEALTHY (good   doctor   hospital   ill   patient)

14 TEACHER (school   pupil   lesson   term   tutor)

15 FRIEND (pal   mate   foe   ally   neighbour)

16 MANY (more   lots   few   crowd   half)

17 WHOLE (entire   part   some   complete   full)

5

Find the three-letter word which can be added to the letters in capitals to make a new word. The new word will complete the sentence sensibly.

Example The cat sprang onto the MO.   <u>USE</u>

18 A baby is an INT. _____

19 A baby goes out in a P. _____

20 A baby CLS on the floor. _____

21 A baby plays with a TLE. _____

22 A baby sits in a HIGHCH. _____

5

Add one letter to the word in capital letters to make a new word. The meaning of the new word is given in the clue.

> **Example** PLAN   simple   <u>plain</u>

23 WAS   an insect   _____

24 HOP   to expect the best   _____

25 LOW   the opposite of fast   _____

26 HAT   to stop   _____

27 RAN   it pours   _____

5

Complete the following expressions by underlining the missing word.

> **Example** Frog is to tadpole as swan is to (duckling, baby, <u>cygnet</u>).

28 Sun is to sunk as pin is to (sink, pin, pan, pink).

29 Fat is to feat as mat is to (mate, team, fate, meat).

30 Bed is to bead as led is to (late, lead, deal, lane).

31 Fin is to find as bin is to (bend, bind, bond, band).

32 Cot is to coat as got is to (good, hot, goat, heat).

33 Ail is to bail as ill is to (sill, will, kill, bill).

6

Write each word backwards and then list them in reverse alphabetical order.

34   boy   but   why   she   sty

_____   _____   _____   _____   _____

1

These words have been written in code, but the codes are not under the right words.

BE	BEG	BIN	BEGIN	BEE
244	24538	24	245	238

Write the correct code for each word.

35 BE   **36** BEG   **37** BIN   **38** BEE   **39** BEGIN

_____   _____   _____   _____   _____

5

If a = 3, b = 2, d = 6, e = 8, f = 10, find the value of:

40 2f − 2a = ___

41 2e − 2b = ___

Sue and Omar wear yellow tops.

Lee and Omar wear green trousers.

Sue and Jess wear brown trousers.

Jess and Lee wear red tops.

Who wears:

42 a yellow top and brown trousers? _____

43 a red top and green trousers? _____

44 a yellow top and green trousers? _____

45 a red top and brown trousers? _____

Now go to the Progress Chart to record your score! Total 45

Paper 5

Which one letter can be added to the front of all of these words to make new words.

Example *c*are *c*at *c*rate *c*all

1 ___arm ___and ___as ___ollow

2 ___old ___hill ___loud ___an

3 ___read ___ream ___ark ___ome

4 ___and ___right ___ear ___each

5 ___rim ___ower ___ride ___lant

5

The train was due in at 10:50. It was 10 minutes late.

6 When did it arrive? _____

I left home at 18:15. It took me 20 minutes to walk to the cinema.

7 When did I get there? _____

13

A pudding takes 50 minutes to cook. I want it to be ready for 13:00.

8 When must I put it into the oven? _____   **3**

If these words were placed in alphabetical order, which word would come first?

9 Monday   Thursday   Wednesday   Friday   Tuesday _____

10 May   January   March   February   April _____

11 giraffe   elephant   mouse   horse   dog _____

12 plane   helicopter   kite   balloon   rocket _____   **4**

Underline one word in the brackets which is most opposite in meaning to the word in capitals.

Example   WIDE   (broad   vague   long   <u>narrow</u>   motorway)

13 WARM   (hot   cold   icy   sun   fine)

14 BLACK   (dark   brown   white   sooty   coal)

15 HIDE   (lost   last   find   skin   search)

16 MORE   (less   many   few   lots   plenty)

17 FIRST   (top   bottom   side   last   enough)   **5**

Underline two words which are made from the same letters.

Example   TAP   PET   <u>TEA</u>   POT   <u>EAT</u>

18 MAUL   PART   MAKE   TRAM   TRAP

19 AGES   ALES   APES   SAGE   SAND

20 LIMP   LEAP   PEEP   PEAL   PEARL

21 WARN   WARM   WARD   WARP   DRAW

22 LATE   LINT   TALE   TILE   FILE   **5**

Remove one letter from the word in capitals to leave a new word. The meaning of the new word is given in the clue.

Example   A U N T   an insect   _ant_

23 ROAD   a stick   _____

24 PINT   something we use when sewing _____

25 TINT   a metal   _____

26 CODE   a type of fish   _____

27 HARM   part of our body   _____   5

Underline the number that completes each sequence.

28 4 is to 16 as 16 is to (72, 64, 60)

29 3 is to 12 as 12 is to (24, 36, 48)

30 32 is to 16 as 16 is to (4, 8, 12)

31 22 is to 11 as 24 is to (11, 12, 14)

32 100 is to 50 as 90 is to (55, 40, 45)   5

These words have been written in code, but the codes are not under the right words.

STOW   SLOW   STEW   LOW   STOLE

9687   96418   9147   9647   147

Write the correct code for each word.

33 STOW   34 SLOW   35 STEW   36 LOW   37 STOLE

_____   _____   _____   _____   _____   5

Underline the word in the brackets which goes best with the words given outside the brackets.

Example   word, paragraph, sentence   (pen, cap, letter, top, stop)

38 bed, bunk, mattress   (drawer, cold, warm, film, pillow)

39 car, lorry, bicycle   (train, road, bus, speed, track)

40 sheep, cows, chickens   (farm, tractor, shed, pigs, bird)

15

41 money, cash, notes   (cheque, bank, lesson, coins, save)

42 mat, tiles, carpet   (curtains, rug, kitchen, sofa, stairs)

Fill in the crosswords so that all the given words are included. You have been given one letter as a clue in each crossword.

43

lost, rust, tear, tool

44

leak, sail, shot, took

45

less, list, seek, tank

Now go to the Progress Chart to record your score!   Total   45

Paper 6

Underline one word in the brackets which is most opposite in meaning to the word in capital letters.

    Example   WIDE   (broad   vague   long   <u>narrow</u>   motorway)

1 SHORT   (length   long   low   metre   up)

2 UP   (saw   went   go   down   tall)

3 YOUNG   (old   clothes   pretty   dress   new)

4 EVEN   (smooth   plain   old   odd   straight)

5 FASTEN   (collar   fix   loosen   tie   bind)

Fill in the crosswords so that all the given words are included. You have been given one letter as a clue in each crossword.

even, idle, iron, noon

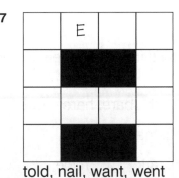

told, nail, want, went

8

bare, hare, bath, rear

3

In each line one word has been muddled up. Rearrange the letters so it fits in with the others.

Example   fly spider moth gnat <u>tan</u>   <u>ant</u>

9 dove lark   wren   tit   low   _____

10 rain   owns mist   hail   fog   _____

11 lump pear   date   lime   apple   _____

12 cake pork   wets   buns   ham   _____

13 goat lamb   deer   loaf   calf   _____

5

Change the first word into the last word by changing one letter at a time and making a new, different word in the middle.

Example   C A S E   <u>C A S H</u>   L A S H

14 LAND   _____   PAID

15 PLAN   _____   CLAP

16 PAID   _____   HAIL

17	WORD	_____	TOLD
18	SILK	_____	TILL

5

Change the first word of the third pair in the same way as the other pairs to give a new word.

Example   bind, hind   bare, hare   but, <u>hut</u>

19	rest, test	road, toad	rent, _____
20	chip, hip	park, ark	mice, _____
21	tear, tar	fear, far	bear, _____
22	bet, beat	set, seat	met, _____
23	and, band	old, bold	all, _____

5

In each line, underline the word which has its letters in alphabetical order.

24	ACE	DEBT	EIGHT	MORE
25	FEW	LIPS	MOST	ROOM

2

Find the three-letter word which can be added to the letters in capitals to make a new word. The new word will complete the sentence sensibly.

Example   The cat sprang onto the MO.   <u>USE</u>

26 A donkey BS.   _____

27 A cock CS.   _____

28 A lion RS.   _____

29 A dog BS.   _____

30 A pig GTS.   _____

5

If the code for LATHER is ABCDEF, what are the codes for the following words?

31 REAL _____   32 LATE _____   33 HEAL _____

What do these codes stand for?

34 DEF _____   35 CEECD _____

The day after tomorrow is Friday.

36 What was the day before yesterday? _____

If Joshua was a year older he would be three times as old as his brother.
His brother is 4.

37 How old is Joshua? _____

I have 20p more than Gita who has 40p less than Mike. Mike has £1.20.

38 How much does Gita have? _____

39 How much do I have? _____   4

Underline the two words which are the odd ones out in the following groups
of words.

| **Example** | black | <u>king</u> | purple | green | <u>house</u> |

40 banana	pear	yellow	purple	apple
41 finger	ring	knee	hat	ear
42 rose	daffodil	daisy	leaf	stem
43 tennis	bat	ball	rugby	swimming	4

Fill in the crosswords so that all the given words are included. You have been
given one letter as a clue in each crossword.

44
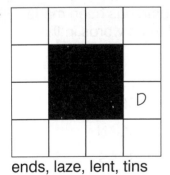
ends, laze, lent, tins

45
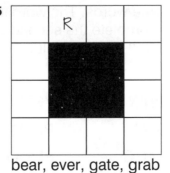
bear, ever, gate, grab   2

Paper 7

Look at these groups of words.

Group A Animals   Group B Colours   Group C Birds

Choose the correct group for each of the words below. Write in the letter.

1 purple ___   2 ferret ___   3 swan ___   4 rabbit ___   5 wren ___   (5)

Underline the pair of words most opposite in meaning.

Example   cup, mug   coffee, milk   <u>hot, cold</u>

6	yes, no	tall, fat	roam, wander
7	happy, glad	teach, learn	blue, sea
8	sorry, cry	quick, run	less, more
9	work, play	high, jump	bright, shining
10	rain, puddle	cat, food	wet, dry

(5)

Underline the one word which **cannot be made** from the letters of the word in capital letters.

Example   S T A T I O N E R Y   stone   tyres   ration   <u>nation</u>   noisy

11	PROFIT	for	toe	top	rot	fit
12	GROWTH	who	got	hot	wet	how
13	COWARD	cod	car	over	row	crow
14	GRAPES	sap	sea	ear	art	peg
15	PATIENT	tap	pin	not	ten	net

(5)

Look at the first group of three words. The word in the middle has been made from the other two words. Complete the second group of three words in the same way, making a new word in the middle.

Example   PAIN   INTO   TOOK   ALSO   <u>SOON</u>   ONLY

16	ALSO	SOON	ONLY	YEAR	_____	CHIN
17	GRIN	GRAB	STAB	PLUM	_____	SCAN
18	MALT	ALSO	SAGO	SMOG	_____	SEAS
19	GATE	GAME	TIME	ROPE	_____	HOSE
20	THIN	MOTH	MOON	STAB	_____	PEAL

(5)

Complete the following sentences by selecting the most sensible word from each group of words given in the brackets. Underline the words selected.

Example The (<u>children</u>, books, foxes) carried the (houses, <u>books</u>, steps) home from the (greengrocer, <u>library</u>, factory).

21 Tom saw a (bird, walrus, rabbit) run down a (chimney, hole, pavement) and into its (drey, burrow, sleep).

22 I feel (cold, lazy, hot) so I must put on a (swim suit, jumper, sandals) then I will feel warmer.

23 The (firework, balloons, streamers) were (burst, inflated, candle) for the party.

24 Clare (wrote, played, sent) a (page, text, letter) to Anya's mobile phone.

25 They (ran, walked, swam) across the (house, class, lake) to the (mist, frog, island).

⬤ 5

Remove one letter from the word in capital letters to leave a new word. The meaning of the new word is given in the clue.

Example A U N T an insect <u>ant</u>

26 BLESS   fewer   _____

27 THEN   a chicken   _____

28 MEAN   male   _____

29 REED   a colour   _____

⬤ 4

Fill in the crosswords so that all the given words are included. You have been given one letter as a clue in each crossword.

30
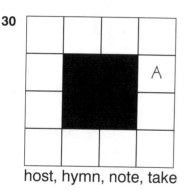
host, hymn, note, take

31
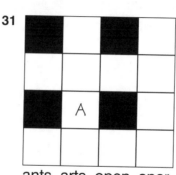
ants, arts, open, spar

⬤ 2

32 If the code for SPIN is ABDE, what is the code for NIPS? _____

33 If the code for RING is CDEF, what is the code for GRIN? _____

34 If the code for SPRIG is ABCDF, what is the code for PRIG? _____

35 If the code for SEAT is 3521, what is the code for TEAS? _____

36 If the code for STEAM is 31526, what is the code for MAST? _____ ⟨5⟩

Fill in the missing number or letters in each sequence.

Example 2 4 6 8 <u>10</u>

37 10 20 40 ___ 160

38 28 24 20 ___ 12

39 19 25 ___ 37 43

40 11 ___ 17 20 23

41 bb bc bd ___ bf ⟨5⟩

Look at this chart.

	English	Art	Maths	Science	ICT
Girls	5	6	2	1	3
Boys	4	2	4	6	3

42 Which subject is liked by twice as many boys as girls? _____

43 Which subject is three times as popular with girls as with boys? _____

44 Which subject is most popular with boys? _____

45 Which subject was liked equally well by boys and girls? _____ ⟨4⟩

Now go to the Progress Chart to record your score!   Total ⟨45⟩

Paper 8

If a = 1, b = 2, c = 3, d = 4, e = 5, f = 6, find the sum of:

1 a + b + c = ___

2 d + e + f = ___

3 2a + b = ___

4 2b + c = ___

5 3a + 2b = ___

6 e + f = ___ ⟨6⟩

Rearrange the muddled letters in capitals to make a proper word. The answer will complete the sentence sensibly.

Example A BEZAR is an animal with stripes. <u>ZEBRA</u>

7 Half of six is HERET. _____

8 Sheep have a thick OLWO coat. _____

9 Don't drop TILTRE in the street. _____

10 The fire crew used AETRW to put out the blaze. _____

11 The tower of the HRCCHU was floodlit. _____ 5

Complete the following sentences by selecting the most sensible word from each group of words given in the brackets. Underline the words selected.

Example The (<u>children</u>, books, foxes) carried the (houses, <u>books</u>, steps) home from the (greengrocer, <u>library</u>, factory).

12 It was (hot, cold, freezing) and she (hated, wanted, disliked) a (pie, hot soup, cold drink) to cool her down.

13 Where is my (shoe, coat, book)? I left it (hiding, running, hanging) in the (shelf, kitchen, cupboard).

14 The (king, soldier, dog) sat in his (car, basket, larder) and (swam, growled, argued). 3

Underline the pair of words most opposite in meaning.

Example cup, mug coffee, milk <u>hot, cold</u>

15 cross, happy   sad, sorry   start, begin

16 neat, tidy   hard, soft   soap, water

17 eat, drink   boil, water   loud, noisy

18 cold, cool   shut, open   oil, tank

19 paper, pencil   pen, write   cry, laugh 5

Look at the first group of three words. The word in the middle has been made from the other two words. Complete the second group of three words in the same way, making a new word in the middle.

Example PAIN INT<u>O</u> TOOK   ALSO <u>SOON</u> ONLY

20 RASH   RAIN   GRIN   CLAN   _____   SLIP

21 POST   STAR   ARMY   POSH   _____   INTO

23

22 CRAG	CREW	EWES	BLUE	_____	ABLE
23 CHAT	CHIN	RAIN	SLAT	_____	SHAM
24 EVEN	VERY	EERY	PLOT	_____	BOOT

◯ 5

Underline the two words which are the odd ones out in the following groups of words.

Example   black   <u>king</u>   purple   green   <u>house</u>

25 cot   sleep   cradle   sing   bed

26 cat   little   water   minute   small

27 road   long   tall   street   fat

28 coat   new   dress   pretty   suit

29 sorry   pleased   happy   glad   old

◯ 5

Fill in the missing letters. The alphabet has been written out to help you.

A B C D E F G H I J K L M N O P Q R S T U V W X Y Z

Example   A B is to C D as P Q is to R S

30 A30 is to B29 as C28 is to _____

31 D20 is to E19 as F18 is to _____

32 100A is to 95B as 90C is to _____

33 A2 is to B3 as C4 is to _____

34 F1 is to E2 as D3 is to _____

◯ 5

Find and underline the two words which need to change places for each sentence to make sense.

Example   She went to <u>letter</u> the <u>write</u>.

35 The drive was parked in the car.

36 We went to holiday for our Scotland.

37 I have to eat my pudding before I can have supper.

38 The shop on my road sweets sells.

39 We are moving our house and selling to Wales.

◯ 5

24

If the code for SECOND is ABCDEF, what are the codes for the following words?

40 ONE _____ **41** CODE _____ **42** ONCE _____

What do these codes stand for?

43 FDEB _____ **44** FDAB _____ **45** ABEF _____ ⟨ 6 ⟩

Now go to the Progress Chart to record your score!   Total ⟨ 45 ⟩

Paper 9

Underline the pair of words most similar in meaning.

Example   come, go   <u>roam, wander</u>   fear, fare

1 fade, tint   blank, empty   hinder, go

2 cut, slit   hit, miss   less, more

3 dry, fine   rich, poor   tea, coffee

4 add, subtract   hole, gap   red, colour

5 tired, weary   hot, cold   forgot, remember ⟨ 5 ⟩

Find the three-letter word which can be added to the letters in capitals to make a new word. The new word will complete the sentence sensibly.

Example   The cat sprang onto the MO.   <u>USE</u>

6 The police will FOL the criminal.   _____

7 A DON is sometimes called an ass.   _____

8 Time to stop for a DR of water.   _____

9 He was pleased to go home from HOSAL.   _____

10 You need a BET to carry your shopping in.   _____ ⟨ 5 ⟩

Find the letter which will end the first word and start the second word.

Example   peac (<u>h</u>) ome

11 gat (__) nds   **12** non (__) ars   **13** min (__) ust

14 ben (__) rim   **15** als (__) dds ⟨ 5 ⟩

Look at the first group of three words. The word in the middle has been made from the other two words. Complete the second group of three words in the same way, making a new word in the middle.

Example PAIN INTO TOOK   ALSO <u>SOON</u> ONLY

16 CLAN   CLOP   STOP   RATS   _____   FISH

17 BAND   BARK   DARK   SLIP   _____   GROW

18 FISH   SHOE   WOES   FAST   _____   TOWN

19 SALT   ALSO   SOOT   PART   _____   CHOP

20 BUSH   BUNK   PINK   STEP   _____   SHOP

○ 5

Complete the following sentences by selecting the most sensible word from each group of words given in the brackets. Underline the words selected.

Example   The (<u>children</u>, books, foxes) carried the (houses, <u>books</u>, steps) home from the (greengrocer, <u>library</u>, factory).

21 She spent a (lot, little, some) of money on all the things she had to (buy, sell, gather) for the big (party, card, mess).

22 The (dog, cow, rabbit) barked furiously at the (burglars, robbing, scare).

23 Tola (buy, bought, bring) her brother a DVD as a (present, surprised, gifts).

24 Don't (run, walk, stand)! You'll (stop, wait, trip) and hurt your (book, friend, knee).

25 The cinema was (dry, packed, fill) for the premiere of the (pictures, movie, showing).

○ 5

If the code for WONDER is 324165, what are the codes for the following words?

26 END _____   27 DEW _____

What do these codes stand for?

28 324 _____   29 3564 _____   30 246 _____

○ 5

If a = 1, b = 2, c = 3, d = 4, e = 5, find the sum of:

31 c + d + b = __   32 2a + 2 = __   33 2c + 2d = __

○ 3

26

It takes 1 hour 30 minutes to do the journey. Fill in the missing times.

34-37

Southby (depart)	Eastby (arrive)
——	12:00
14:30	——
16:10	——
——	18:30

4

If the letters in the following words are arranged in alphabetical order, which letter comes in the middle?

38 FAIRY ——

39 PLACE ——

40 LIGHT ——

41 TEACH ——

4

Worzles and Dingbats like to eat leaves and shoots.

Sninks and Dingbats like snails and slugs.

Worzles and Wigglers like weeds and grass.

Wigglers and Sninks like flies and berries.

42 Who likes berries but not weeds? ——————

43 Who likes leaves, shoots and slugs? ——————

44 Who likes snails and flies? ——————

45 Who likes weeds, grass, flies and berries? ——————

4

Now go to the Progress Chart to record your score! Total 45

Paper 10

Underline the two words which are the odd ones out in the following groups of words.

Example black <u>king</u> purple green <u>house</u>

1 child   wash   clean   parent   bath

2 circle   newspaper   ring   hoop   comic

3	grey	yellow	apple	blue	cherry
4	jeans	turban	white	brown	sweater
5	bench	ball	seat	chair	bat

Find the three-letter word which can be added to the letters in capitals to make a new word. The new word will complete the sentence sensibly.

Example   The cat sprang onto the MO.   <u>USE</u>

6 The CH he sat on was hard.   _____

7 The CSE of the river was long and winding.   _____

8 The show INS at eight.   _____

9 At the start of the play the ORS appeared on the stage. _____

10 The BN dog ran wildly after the ball.   _____

Find the letter which will end the first word and start the second word.

Example   peac (<u>h</u>) ome

11 lan (__) are   12 fea (__) ule

13 gon (__) ver   14 sto (__) ond

15 cla (__) hite

These words have been written in code, but the codes are not under the right words.

AT	THE	CHAT	HAT	ACT
2315	15	125	534	315

Write the correct code for each word.

16 AT   17 THE   18 CHAT

_____   _____   _____

19 HAT   20 ACT

_____   _____

Paper 1

1. alley, lane
2. heavy, weighty
3. bite, nip
4. correct, right
5. closed, shut
6. EVE
7. HOE
8. ILL
9. HOW
10. FOR
11. below
12. inside
13. forgot
14. fingertip
15. handsome
16. pant
17. tear
18. tried
19. pain
20. stab
21. J
22. 6H
23. DEG
24. PDE
25. 6GH
26.

H	O	M	E
I			D
N			I
T	E	N	T

27.

T	E	R	M
I			O
M			S
E	N	D	S

28.

W	I	S	H
A			E
G			A
S	H	I	P

29. 18
30. 2000
31. 8
32. 6.5
33. 20
34. 6
35. 573
36. 751
37. 915
38. 933
39. 135
40. SPEAR
41. APPEAR
42. 15 minutes
43. 75 minutes
44. 30 minutes
45. 30 minutes

Paper 2

1. bright
2. fast
3. chuckle
4. new
5. easy
6. bottom, thin
7. dark, dirty
8. tall, found
9. empty, smooth
10. open, slow
11. d
12. e
13. t
14. k
15. t
16.

C	A	M	P
A			L
T			U
S	H	A	M

17.

B	E	N	D
E			A
A			R
M	I	L	K

18.

B	A	N	K
E			I
A			N
R	I	N	G

19. bedside
20. underground
21. inform
22. outlaw
23. forgive
24. PINE
25. COME
26. COPE
27. MATE
28. GOLD
29. 5632
30. 586
31. TOP
32. TOSS
33. ERR
34. walls
35. water
35. buildings
37. a stove
38. students
39. MEAT, TEAM
40. TEN, NET
41. LAST, SALT
42. far
43. ham
44. round
45. tan

Paper 3

1. crowd, concert
2. enlarge, expand
3. harbour, pier
4. weak, ill
5. swim, dive
6. ARM
7. EAR
8. JAM
9. COT
10. TEN
11. p
12. b
13. s
14. m
15. s
16. trout
17. noise
18. thick
19. plate
20. sport

Bond Verbal Reasoning Assessment Papers 8-9 years

21

```
M I S T
A . R .
R . I .
K E E P
```

22

```
H A L F
A . I .
R . R .
D A T E
```

23

```
P A R T
E . I .
A . D .
R I P E
```

24	12
25	6
26	36
27	54
28	343
29	722
30	247
31	727
32	72
33	46
34	6
35	7
36	6
37	dear
38	flow
39	eaten
40	need
41	got
42	ant
43	cry
44	dint
45	flow

Paper 4

1	tail, dog
2	sister, mother
3	bed, book
4	cake, party
5	office, bus
6	seaweed
7	sandcastle

8	workshop
9	handshake
10	underwater

11

```
P O R T
A . . O
R . . R
K E E N
```

12

```
H E A L
O . . A
L . . Z
E A S Y
```

13	ill
14	pupil
15	foe
16	few
17	part
18	FAN
19	RAM
20	RAW
21	RAT
22	AIR
23	wasp
24	hope
25	slow
26	halt
27	rain
28	pink
29	meat
30	lead
31	bind
32	goat
33	bill
34	yts, yob, yhw, tub, ehs
35	24
36	245
37	238
38	244
39	24538
40	14
41	12
42	Sue
43	Lee
44	Omar
45	Jess

Paper 5

1	h
2	c
3	d
4	b
5	p
6	11:00
7	18:35
8	12:10
9	Friday
10	April
11	dog
12	balloon
13	cold
14	white
15	find
16	less
17	last
18	PART, TRAP
19	AGES, SAGE
20	LEAP, PEAL
21	WARD, DRAW
22	LATE, TALE
23	rod
24	pin
25	tin
26	cod
27	arm
28	64
29	48
30	8
31	12
32	45
33	9647
34	9147
35	9687
36	147
37	96418
38	pillow
39	bus
40	pigs
41	coins
42	rug

43

```
T O O L
E . . O
A . . S
R U S T
```

44

```
S A I L
H ▓ E
O ▓ A
T O O K
```

45
```
L E S S
I ▓ E
S ▓ E
T A N K
```

Paper 6

1 long
2 down
3 old
4 odd
5 loosen

6

```
I R O N
D ▓ O
L ▓ O
E V E N
```

7
```
W E N T
A ▓ O
N A I L
T ▓ D
```

8
```
B A T H
A ▓ A
R E A R
E ▓ E
```

9 owl
10 snow
11 plum
12 stew
13 foal
14 LAID
15 CLAN
16 PAIL
17 WOLD
18 SILL
19 tent
20 ice
21 bar
22 meat
23 ball

24 ACE
25 MOST
26 RAY
27 ROW
28 OAR
29 ARK
30 RUN
31 FEBA
32 ABCE
33 DEBA
34 HER
35 TEETH
36 Monday
37 11
38 80p
39 £1.00
40 yellow, purple
41 ring, hat
42 leaf, stem
43 bat, ball

44

```
L A Z E
E ▓ N
N ▓ D
T I N S
```

45
```
G R A B
A ▓ E
T ▓ A
E V E R
```

Paper 7

1 B
2 A
3 C
4 A
5 C
6 yes, no
7 teach, learn
8 less, more
9 work, play
10 wet, dry
11 toe
12 wet
13 over
14 art

15 not
16 ARCH
17 PLAN
18 MOSS
19 ROSE
20 PEST
21 rabbit, hole, burrow
22 cold, jumper
23 balloons, inflated
24 sent, text
25 swam, lake, island
26 less
27 hen
28 man
29 red

30

```
H O S T
Y ▓ A
M ▓ K
N O T E
```

31

```
▓ S ▓ A
O P E N
▓ A ▓ T
A R T S
```

32 EDBA
33 FCDE
34 BCDF
35 1523
36 6231
37 80
38 16
39 31
40 14
41 be
42 Maths
43 Art
44 Science
45 ICT

Paper 8

1 6
2 15
3 4
4 7
5 7
6 11

Bond Verbal Reasoning Assessment Papers 8-9 years

7	THREE	6	LOW	6	AIR
8	WOOL	7	KEY	7	OUR
9	LITTER	8	INK	8	BEG
10	WATER	9	PIT	9	ACT
11	CHURCH	10	ASK	10	ROW
12	hot, wanted, cold drink	11	e	11	d
13	coat, hanging, cupboard	12	e	12	r
14	dog, basket, growled	13	d	13	e
15	cross, happy	14	t	14	p
16	hard, soft	15	o	15	w
17	eat, drink	16	RASH	16	15
18	shut, open	17	SLOW	17	534
19	cry, laugh	18	STOW	18	2315
20	CLIP	19	ARCH	19	315
21	SHIN	20	STOP	20	125
22	BLAB	21	lot, buy, party	21	fork
23	SLAM	22	dog, burglars	22	E
24	LOOT	23	bought, present	23	spade, beach, castle
25	sleep, sing	24	run, trip, knee	24	fixed, pipe
26	cat, water	25	packed, movie	25	heard, burglar, house
27	road, street	26	641	26	help, lift, table
28	new, pretty	27	163	27	owl, hooted, wood
29	sorry, old	28	WON	28	w
30	D27	29	WREN	29	b
31	G17	30	ONE	30	f
32	85D	31	9	31	o
33	D5	32	4	32	c
34	C4	33	14	33	SORT
35	drive, car	34–37	Southby depart 10:30	34	BULK
36	holiday, Scotland		Eastby arrive 16:00	35	STAB
37	pudding, supper		Eastby arrive 17:40	36	HOPE
38	sweets, sells		Southby depart 17:00	37	EASY
39	moving, selling	38	I	38	loud
40	DEB	39	E	39	cub
41	CDFB	40	I	40	shin
42	DECB	41	E	41	lie
43	DONE	42	Sninks	42	pan
44	DOSE	43	Dingbats	43	tools, stool
45	SEND	44	Sninks	44	slip, lips
		45	Wigglers	45	toga, goat

Paper 9

1 blank, empty
2 cut, slit
3 dry, fine
4 hole, gap
5 tired, weary

Paper 10

1 child, parent
2 newspaper, comic
3 apple, cherry
4 white, brown
5 ball, bat

Paper 11

1

2

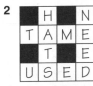

	H		N	
T	A	M	E	
		T	E	
U	S	E	D	

3

C	A	F	E	
A			I	
R	U	S	H	
T			H	

4 yawned, tired, bed
5 bike, swerved, road
6 climbed, window, castle
7 lights, dark
8 danced, rhythm
9 hairdresser, dentist
10 cage, pool
11 newspaper, dictionary
12 rice, bread
13 candle, cake
14 KEGCK
15 KGCE
16 ACI
17 IGCK
18 TRAP
19 REAP
20 PART
21 mist
22 all
23 rake
24 boat
25 burden, load
26 kind, thoughtful
27 expect, hope
28 little, small
29 hide, conceal
30 SHE
31 RAN
32 KIN
33 AGE
34 HIT
35 e
36 h
37 k
38 e
39 e
40 AIR
41 BE

42 SEA
43 SAND
44 OUT
45 IN

Paper 12

1–5 Give one mark for each two right answers:
cricket C, peas D, axe A, drum B, saw A, guitar B, potatoes D, hammer A, piano B, football C

6 w
7 s
8 w
9 t
10 f
11 outfit
12 beside
13 farewell
14 afterwards
15 checkout
16 boy
17 doctors
18 lamb
19 sheep
20 burrow

21

	S		S	
N	E	W	S	
A			A	
G	O	N	E	

22

		R		A
	H	E	L	D
		A		D
A	P	E	S	

23

C	A	S	T	
H		H		
E	V	E	N	
W		D		

24 G
25 21
26 February
27 December
28 @ ÷ +

29 × ÷ @
30 − ÷ ×
31 WAR
32 STAR
33 Mr Young's age: 30
34 Joshua's age: 2
35 Joshua's age:10
36 race, teacher, whistle
37 birds, seed, garden
38 flowers, pot, door
39 table, forks, knives
40 cars, work, morning
41 outside, cold
42 apple, salad
43 holiday, Christmas
44 road, car
45 moon, window

Paper 13

1

S		C		
P	E	A	S	
I		L		
T	I	M	E	

2

	T		H	
T	A	L	E	
	I		R	
A	L	S	O	

3

G	I	R	L	
A		U		
T	I	D	Y	
E		E		

4 unhappy, sad
5 sharp, pointed
6 loud, noisy
7 cheap, inexpensive
8 terror, fear
9 sad
10 starve
11 still
12 dirty
13 hinder
14 O
15 N
16 E
17 F

Bond Verbal Reasoning Assessment Papers 8-9 years

18 rear
19 sore
20 late
21 tale
22 sing
23 ride
24 6413
25 1563
26 463
27 NOON
28 SOON
29 28
30 34
31 19
32 red
33 need
34 rot
35 none
36 star
37 HAIR
38 UNDER
39 SHIP
40 UP
41 CART
42 1
43 3
44 2
45 4

Paper 14

1 PINK
2 GREY
3 NAVY
4 MAUVE
5 BROWN
6 hotplate
7 rainbow
8 toothache
9 football
10 fireplace
11 moist
12 flower
13 front
14 trots
15 ground
16 go, come

17 night, day
18 full, empty
19 tall, short
20 play, work
21
22
23
24 CG
25 6F
26 FD
27 54
28 47
29 ÷ % − +
30 + % ÷
31 × % ÷
32 MAST
33 ARMS
34 de
35 df
36 ef
37 three
38 Sally, Annie
39 Kim
40 Tuesday, Friday, Sunday
41 tired, exhausted
42 swerve, dodge
43 mean, stingy
44 soldiers, troops
45 double, twice

Paper 15

1 grass, lawn
2 wash, dry
3 house, cottage
4 plate, dish

5 glove, hat
6 light
7 wing
8 ran
9 cat
10 hat
11
12
13
14 sip
15 feat
16 wets
17 race
18 flat
19 6
20 7
21 12
22 birthday, mother, cake
23 chips, fish
24 night, wet, windy
25 eat, cake, poisoned
26 people, seen, city
27 + − − +
28 ÷ / × −
29 − + × ÷ − /
30 ONION
31 TINT
32 hold
33 final
34 rich
35 stake
36 near, far
37 save, spend
38 ugly, pretty
39 friend, enemy
40 quiet, noisy

41 year, sea
42 school, house
43 had, I
44 ways, both
45 seeds, flowers

41 feed
42 face
43 bead
44 fade
45 add

41 seed
42 icy
43 slide
44 lift
45 tilt

Paper 16

1 tired, sit
2 sister, dance, boyfriend
3 left, purse, shop
4 ring, ambulance, mobile
5 supper, moon, sky
6 trees
7 a tail
8 man
9 with patients
10 roots
11 December
12 eleven
13 individual
14 release
15 alabaster
16 $+ - \times \div /$
17 $\div + + - \times$
18 $+ \div - \times$
19 DALE
20 DEED
21 crate
22 sold
23 hole
24 hard
25 super
26 children
27 pens
28 noises
29 bungalow
30 box
31 beginning, end
32 open, closed
33 high, low
34 strong, weak
35 quiet, loud
36 END
37 NUT
38 ODE
39 EAR
40 WAR

Paper 17

1 10
2 11
3 11
4 8
5 3
6 heavy, light
7 here, there
8 whisper, shout
9 late, early
10 glad, sad
11 ACE
12 ROT
13 TON
14 ROW
15 JOY
16 d
17 e
18 t
19 k
20 t
21 NEST
22 CHIN
23 BASH
24 BEAT
25 BEST
26 help, aid
27 ruin, spoil
28 angry, cross
29 hear, listen
30 price, cost
31 BAND
32 CLASS
33 DRUMS
34 PIANO
35 NOISE
36 49
37 30
38 28
39 250
40 76

Paper 18

1–5 Give one mark for each two correct answers: whisk A, camel D, Dutch B, scales A, gull C, German B, lamb D, recipe A, goose C, French B
6 ATE
7 CAR
8 ARE
9 WAS
10 TEA
11 d
12 t
13 g
14 p
15 e
16
17
18 seat
19 list
20 moat
21 heat
22 than
23 $- / \times$
24 $\$ = / @ \times$
25 $= / @ + /$
26 TAG
27 GATE
28 B
29 D
30 A

31 C
32 bead
33 E
34 K
35 S
36 words, spelling, school
37 writer, study, book
38 landed, broke, applause
39 sister, boyfriend, birthday
40 spent, weekend, lines
41 leave, depart
42 bitter, sour
43 calm, peaceful
44 sweep, brush
45 grateful, thankful

Paper 19

1 same
2 say
3 let
4 beloved
5 tree
6 OUR
7 RAN
8 BAN
9 HAD
10 PEN
11 e
12 t
13 e
14 t
15 o
16 M
17 10J
18 IJL
19 QEF
20 5IJ
21

22

23

24 CASTLE
25 ANYONE
26 PIRATE
27 CINEMA
28 SHOPPING
29 145
30 541
31 144
32 146
33 6417
34 queen, castle, crown
35 clock, on time school
36 winter, snow, sledging
37 ill, medicine, better
38 nap
39 send
40 poke
41 soil
42 aunt
43 16
44 18
45 28

Paper 20

1 D50
2 35D
3 DW
4 GH
5 T
6 11
7 32
8 20
9 18
10 35
11 425
12 266
13 4275
14 4751
15 256
16 26
17 13
18 16
19 INCH, CHIN
20 BRUSH, SHRUB
21 NEAR, EARN
22 CLASP, SCALP
23 feet, teeth
24 pig, dog
25 reason, fault
26 brief, short
27 glad, happy
28 yell, scream
29 talk, speak
30 see, look
31 BAT
32 HIP
33 OAR
34 LOW
35 RED
36 I
37 t
38 d
39 t
40 e
41 helpless
42 setback
43 matchstick
44 message
45 indoors

21 four   fork   fire   fall   feel

If these words were placed in alphabetical order, which word would come fourth?

_____

22 If the letters in the following word are arranged in alphabetical order, which letter comes in the middle?

CHASE _____

    2

Complete the following sentences by selecting the most sensible word from each group of words given in the brackets. Underline the words selected.

Example   The (<u>children</u>, books, foxes) carried the (houses, <u>books</u>, steps) home from the (greengrocer, <u>library</u>, factory).

23 Mai took her (spoon, spade, hoe) to the (garden, beach, park) to build a (bridge, castle, palace).

24 The workman (knocked, fixed, tied) the (string, pipe, paper) in the bathroom.

25 No one (heard, wanted, bought) the (washing, burglar, road) enter the (kennel, fridge, house).

26 Can you (wait, hinder, help) me (empty, lift, buy) this box onto the (lawn, table, dog)?

27 The (monster, policeman, owl) (hooted, whispered, sang) in the (cupboard, hall, wood).

    5

Which one letter can be added to the front of all these words to make new words?

Example   <u>c</u>are   <u>c</u>at   <u>c</u>rate   <u>c</u>all

28 __hale   __rap   __in   __art

29 __lame   __right   __one   __urn

30 __lint   __ray   __rank   __lea

31 __pen   __at   __pal   __range

32 __lip   __limb   __heat   __harm

    5

Look at the first group of three words. The word in the middle has been made from the other two words. Complete the second group of three words in the same way, making a new word in the middle of the group.

Example   PAIN   INTO   TOOK   ALSO   <u>SOON</u>   ONLY

33 VEST   VEIN   PAIN   SOME   _____   TART

34 HARP   PART   PORT   GULP   _____   BARK

35 MASH   SHIP   TRIP   FIST   _____   GRAB

36 SELL   SEAT   BEAT   HOME   _____   RIPE

37 MARK   ARMS   HEMS   PEAL   _____   BUSY   (5

Remove one letter from the word in capital letters to leave a new word. The meaning of the new word is given in the clue.

Example   A U N T   an insect   <u>ant</u>

38 CLOUD   not quiet   _____

39 CLUB   a baby bear   _____

40 SHINE   part of the leg   _____

41 LIFE   a fib   _____

42 PANT   used for cooking   _____   (5

43–45 In each list of words, the letters of one word have been jumbled up. Underline it and write it correctly.

FURNITURE   PARTS OF THE BODY   ANIMALS

   piano   slip   mare

   tools   nose   frog

   table   eyes   toga

   _____   _____   _____   (3

Paper 11

Fill in the crosswords so that all the given words are included. You have been given one letter as a clue in each crossword.

1

ever, done, opal, late

2

hats, need, tame, used

3

café, cart, fish, rush

3

Complete the following sentences by selecting the most sensible word from each group of words given in the brackets. Underline the words selected.

Example   The (<u>children</u>, books, foxes) carried the (houses, <u>books</u>, steps) home from the (greengrocer, <u>library</u>, factory).

4   The old lady (smiled, yawned, laughed) because she was (tired, worried, ill) and wanted to go to (hospital, bed, play).

5   The (bike, ship, bed) (fell, swerved, ran) across the (pond, road, door).

6   He carefully (waited, cooked, climbed) through the (roof, garden, window) into the (zoo, kennel, castle).

7   She turned on the (lights, curtains, towels) as it was getting (light, dark, sunny).

8   Alex (hum, danced, clap) to the (rhythm, rhyme, tone) of the music.

5

31

Change one word so that the sentence makes sense. Underline the word you are taking out and write your new word on the line.

Example   I waited in line to buy a <u>book</u> to see the film.   *ticket*

9   I had a toothache so my mother took me to the hairdresser. _____

10 The swimming cage in my town has two diving boards. _____

11 When I asked my mum what a word meant she told me to look it up in the newspaper. _____

12 For lunch I like a cheese sandwich on brown rice and an apple. _____

13 My birthday candle this year is going to be chocolate sponge. _____   ⑤

If the code for PARENT is ACEGIK, what are the codes for the following words?

14 TREAT _____   15 TEAR _____

16 PAN _____   17 NEAT _____

What do these codes stand for?

18 KECA _____   19 EGCA _____   20 ACEK _____   ⑦

Change the first word of the third pair in the same way as the other pairs to give a new word.

Example   bind, hind   bare, hare   but, <u>hut</u>

21 light, might   line, mine   list, _____

22 hair, air   hand, and   ball, _____

23 beach, reach   best, rest   bake, _____

24 oil, boil   old, bold   oat, _____   ④

Underline the pair of words most similar in meaning.

Example   come, go   <u>roam, wander</u>   fear, fare

25 help, hinder   hate, horrid   burden, load

26 kind, thoughtful   come, go   top, hill

27 low, slight   expect, hope   come, depart

28 little, small   fly, down   top, bottom

29 last, ever   one, once   hide, conceal   ⑤

Find the three-letter word which can be added to the letters in capitals to make a new word. The new word will complete the sentence sensibly.

Example The cat sprang onto the MO. <u>USE</u>

30 We keep the mower in the garden D. _____

31 The flowers are a bright OGE colour. _____

32 She peeled the apple and composted the S. _____

33 Some PS of the book were torn. _____

34 I like the yolk but not the WE of egg. _____

5

Find the letter which will end the first word and start the second word.

Example peac (<u>h</u>) o m e

35 lon (__) ggs

36 bat (__) orn

37 mar (__) nit

38 pan (__) lse

39 mar (__) els

5

Find a word that can be put in front of each of the following words to make new, compound words.

Example CAST   FALL   WARD   POUR   <u>DOWN</u>

40 PORT	BAG	SHIP	CRAFT	_____
41 CAUSE	HIND	NEATH	COME	_____
42 SIDE	SHELL	GULL	BED	_____
43 CASTLE	PIT	STORM	PAPER	_____
44 SIDE	STRETCH	SHINE	RIGHT	_____
45 SIDE	CREASE	DOOR	LAND	_____

6

Paper 12

1–5 Look at these groups of words.

Group A Tools   Group B Musical instruments
Group C Sports or games   Group D Vegetables

Choose the correct group for each of the words below. Write in the letter.

cricket __   peas __   axe __   drum __   saw __

guitar __   potatoes __   hammer __   piano __   football __

5

Find the letter which will end the first word and start the second word.

Example   peac (h) ome

6 blo (__) ish   **7** pas (__) pin   **8** sho (__) ind

9 mus (__) idy   **10** puf (__) eed

5

Underline two words, one from each group, that go together to form a new word. The word in the first group always comes first.

Example   (hand, green, for)   (light, house, sure)

11 (in, of, out)   (fit, ill, well)

12 (was, be, do)   (front, side, back)

13 (say, fare, end)   (ill, gone, well)

14 (before, when, after)   (come, wards, wet)

15 (check, pencil, pen)   (down, side, out)

5

Complete the following expressions by underlining the missing word.

Example   Frog is to tadpole as swan is to (duckling, baby, cygnet).

16 Aunt is to uncle as girl is to (boy, cousin, son).

17 Pupils are to teachers as patients are to (surgery, doctors, accident).

18 Dog is to puppy as sheep is to (ram, lamb, cow).

19 Crowd is to people as flock is to (sheep, pigs, cows).

20 Pig is to sty as rabbit is to (drey, burrow, nest).

5

Fill in the crosswords so that all the given words are included. You have been given one letter as a clue in each crossword.

21

gone, news, snag, swan

22

adds, apes, held, reap

23

cast, chew, even, shed

24 If the first five letters of the alphabet were removed, which would be the second letter of those left? Circle the correct letter.

   E   H   G   F

25 How many letters would there be in this alphabet? Circle the correct number.

   20   21   22

26 Which month of the year begins with the sixth letter of the usual alphabet? _____

27 Which month of the year begins with the fourth letter? _____

If the code for STRAW is + − × ÷ @, what are the codes for the following words?

28 WAS _____   29 RAW _____   30 TAR _____

What do these codes stand for?

31 @ ÷ × _____   32 + − ÷ × _____

35

33–35 Mr Young was 25 when Joshua was born. Complete the table.

Mr Young's age	27		35
Joshua's age		5	

Complete the following sentences by selecting the most sensible word from each group of words given in the brackets. Underline the words selected.

Example The (children, books, foxes) carried the (houses, books, steps) home from the (greengrocer, library, factory).

36 The (race, film, job) started when the (teacher, doctor, baker) blew her (crown, pencil, whistle).

37 My mum feeds the (birds, fish, cats) each morning by putting some (jam, seed, cake) out in the (car, bin, garden).

38 In our garden we have some (swings, rocks, flowers) in a (cup, pot, dish) that sit near the back (lake, road, door).

39 Jenny set the (chair, table, television) for supper by laying out the (books, pots, forks) and (pans, knives, apples).

40 The noise of the (bikes, trees, cars) as people go to (work, sleep, play) in the (morning, holiday, sun) wakes me.

Find and underline the two words which need to change places for each sentence to make sense.

Example She went to letter the write.

41 It is too outside to go cold today.

42 The fruit apple was made with grapes, pear and salad.

43 My aunt and uncle come and spend every holiday Christmas with us.

44 The police officer told the man to move his road because it was blocking the car.

45 Sometimes when I look out of my moon at night I can see the window.

Paper 13

Fill in the crosswords so that all the given words are included. You have been given one letter as a clue in each crossword.

1

calm, peas, spit, time

2

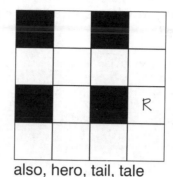

also, hero, tail, tale

3

gate, girl, rude, tidy

3

Underline the pair of words most similar in meaning.

Example   come, go   <u>roam, wander</u>   fear, fare

4 unhappy, sad   many, few   speak, listen

5 accept, refuse   divide, add   sharp, pointed

6 buy, sell   throw, catch   loud, noisy

7 cheap, inexpensive   generous, mean   rough, smooth

8 feeble, strong   give, take   terror, fear

5

Underline one word in the brackets which is most opposite in meaning to the word in capitals.

Example   WIDE   (broad   vague   long   <u>narrow</u>   motorway)

9 CHEERFUL   (happy   pleased   sad   joyful   thoughtful)

10 EAT   (meals   starve   hungry   food   dine)

37

11	MOVING	(jump still run skip slow)
12	CLEAN	(tint washed dirty dyed spill)
13	HELP	(aid assist hinder flop earn)

5

If the letters in the following words are arranged in alphabetical order, which letter comes in the middle?

14 POUND   ———

15 TRAIN   ———

16 READS   ———

17 AFTER   ———

4

Remove one letter from the word in capital letters to leave a new word. The meaning of the new word is given in the clue.

Example   A U N T   an insect   <u>ant</u>

18 DREAR   at the back   ———

19 SHORE   painful   ———

20 PLATE   opposite of early   ———

21 STALE   a story   ———

22 SINGE   make a tune with the voice   ———

23 PRIDE   to go on horseback   ———

6

If the code for SEASON is 135146, what are the codes for the following words?

24 NOSE ———   25 SANE ———   26 ONE ———

What do these codes stand for?

27 6446 ———   28 1446 ———

5

The pegs on one side of a cloakroom are numbered 1 to 20. On the other side they are numbered 21 to 40. 1 is opposite 21.

29 What number peg is opposite 8?   —

30 What number peg is opposite 14?   —

31 What number peg is opposite 39?   —

3

Underline the one word which **cannot be made** from the letters of the word in capital letters.

Example   S T A T I O N E R Y   stone   tyres   ration   <u>nation</u>   noisy

32 FLOWER   low   few   red   row   fro

33 WANDER   and   dear   draw   need   read

34 CURATE   eat   ate   rot   car   care

35 MEANING   nine   man   men   none   mane

36 FASTEN   east   sat   neat   fate   star

5

Find a word that can be put in front of each of the following words to make new, compound words.

Example   CAST   FALL   WARD   POUR   <u>DOWN</u>

37 PIN   NET   SLIDE   DRYER   _____

38 GO   HAND   MINE   RATE   _____

39 MATE   YARD   OWNER   SHAPE   _____

40 ROAR   SET   RIGHT   WARD   _____

41 WHEEL   LOAD   RIDGE   HORSE   _____

5

Houses 1 and 2 have green doors.

Houses 2 and 3 have brown windows.

Houses 1 and 4 have blue windows.

Houses 4 and 3 have red doors.

Which house has:

42 a green door and blue windows?   _____

43 a red door and brown windows?   _____

44 a green door and brown windows?   _____

45 a red door and blue windows?   _____

4

Rearrange the muddled letters in capitals to make proper words. They are all colours.

1 KPIN _____   2 YREG _____

3 YVAN _____   4 AEUVM _____

5 NORWB _____

Underline two words, one from each group, that go together to form a new word. The word in the first group always comes first.

Example (hand, <u>green</u>, for)   (light, <u>house</u>, sure)

6 (old, hot, white)   (paper, plate, petal)

7 (rain, snow, wet)   (bow, arch, building)

8 (blood, tooth, pain)   (hurt, sore, ache)

9 (big, leg, foot)   (ball, park, shoe)

10 (fire, water, sea)   (switch, alarm, place)

Add one letter to the word in capital letters to make a new word. The meaning of the new word is given in the clue.

Example PLAN   simple   _plain_

11 MIST   to be damp   _____

12 LOWER   grows in the garden _____

13 FONT   opposite of back   _____

14 ROTS   a horse does this   _____

15 ROUND   land   _____

Underline the two words, one from each group, which are the most opposite in meaning.

Exam (dawn, <u>early</u>, wake)   (<u>late</u>, stop, sunrise)

16 (go, back, front)   (here, for, come)

17 (moon, night, dark)   (day, shadow, dawn)

18 (full, small, big)   (over, tiny, empty)

19 (big, height, tall)   (large, short, huge)

20 (play, lazy, good)   (hard, cross, work)

Fill in the crosswords so that all the given words are included. You have been given one letter as a clue in each crossword.

21

asks, sago, seat, spot

22

coop, hear, hope, spar

23

cart, chip, iron, root

Give the missing numbers and letters in the following sequences. The alphabet has been written out to help you.

A B C D E F G H I J K L M N O P Q R S T U V W X Y Z

	Example	CQ	DQ	EP	FP	GO
24	AE	BF	___	DH	EI	
25	4D	5E	___	7G	8H	
26	DB	EC	___	GE	HF	
27	76	65	___	43	32	
28	29	38	___	56	65	

If the code for MASTER is + − × ÷ % @, what are the codes for the following words?

29 TEAM _____   **30** MET _____   **31** SET _____

What do these codes stand for?

32 $+ - \times \div$ _____

33 $- @ + \times$ _____

If a = 2, b = 3, c = 4, d = 5, e = 6, f = 7, g = 8, h = 9, find the sum of these questions. Give your answers as letters.

34	b a	**35**	b c	**36**	c c
	+ a c		+ a b		+ a b
	_____		_____		_____

Some children do a paper round.

Mike does Wednesday and Saturday. He sometimes does Monday as well.

Sally does Monday and Thursday. She never helps on Saturday.

Annie does Monday and Wednesday. She sometimes helps on Thursday.

Kim does Thursday and Saturday. She sometimes helps on Wednesday.

37 How many different children might work on Wednesday? _____

38 Who usually works on Monday? _____

39 Who works on Thursday but not Monday? _____

40 Which days of the week do none of the children work?

_____

Underline the pair of words most similar in meaning.

Example	come, go	<u>roam, wander</u>	fear, fare
41 unhappy, cross	tired, exhausted	run, skip
42 crawl, walk	sit, stand	swerve, dodge
43 mean, stingy	generous, poor	give, receive
44 army, navy	sea, harbour	soldiers, troops
45 first, last	first, tenth	double, twice

Underline the two words which are the odd ones out in the following groups of words.

Example   black   <u>king</u>   purple   green   <u>house</u>

1 green   grass   blue   lawn   red

2 wash   friend   pal   dry   mate

3 cod   house   salmon   herring   cottage

4 plate   cheese   dish   bread   butter

5 shoe   glove   boot   hat   sandal

5

Remove one letter from the word in capital letters to leave a new word. The meaning of the new word is given in the clue.

Example   A U N T   an insect   <u>ant</u>

6 FLIGHT   not heavy   _____

7 SWING   part of a bird   _____

8 RANK   walked fast   _____

9 COAT   a pet   _____

10 HEAT   you wear it on your head   _____

5

Fill in the crosswords so that all the given words are included. You have been given one letter as a clue in each crossword.

11

heat, pony, rain, ship

12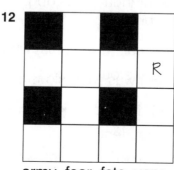

army, fear, fete, very

43

13

dote, late, wide, will

3

Change the first word of the third pair in the same way as the other pairs to give a new word.

    Example   bind, hind   bare, hare   but, <u>hut</u>

14 crane, cane   plot, pot   ship, _____

15 pat, peat   wed, weed   fat, _____

16 rats, star   peek, keep   stew, _____

17 lime, mile   rite, tire   care, _____

18 sit, sat   clip, clap   flit, _____

5

If $a = 1$, $b = 2$, $c = 3$, $d = 4$, find the value of the following:

19 $a \times b \times c =$ __   20 $(b \times d) - a =$ __   21 $c \times d =$ __

3

Complete the following sentences by selecting the most sensible word from each group of words given in the brackets. Underline the words selected.

    Example   The (<u>children</u>, books, foxes) carried the (houses, <u>books</u>, steps) home from the (greengrocer, <u>library</u>, factory).

22 On my (day, morning, birthday) my (dog, cat, mother) makes me a special (biscuit, cake, bun).

23 The girl liked to eat (cereal, milk, chips) with her (table, soup, fish).

24 The (night, pond, moon) was (wet, slow, heavy) and (sunny, dry, windy).

25 Don't (burn, bake, eat) the (stone, king, cake). It's been (baked, poisoned, lost)!

26 Few (sheep, goats, people) have ever (seen, grazed, stolen) the ruined (hedge, pond, city).

5

If the code for POTION is $+ - \times \div - /$, what are the codes for the following words?

27 POOP _____

28 INTO _____

29 OPTION _____

What do these codes stand for?

30 $- / \div - /$ _____

31 $\times \div / \times$ _____

5

Underline the word in brackets closest in meaning to the word in capitals.

Example UNHAPPY (unkind death laughter <u>sad</u> friendly)

32 CONTAIN (order help hold drop box)

33 LAST (first final try start ending)

34 WEALTHY (poor money banker rich cheque)

35 POST (wood stand box sign stake)

4

Underline the two words, one from each group, which are the most opposite in meaning.

Example (dawn, <u>early</u>, wake) (<u>late</u>, stop, sunrise)

36 (help, near, hope) (far, away, gone)

37 (save, money, box) (shop, keeper, spend)

38 (paint, brush, ugly) (colour, pretty, box)

39 (pat, like, friend) (unkind, sad, enemy)

40 (sound, quiet, song) (noisy, voice, sang)

5

Find and underline the two words which need to change places for each sentence to make sense.

Example She went to <u>letter</u> the <u>write</u>.

41 We went to the year for our holiday this sea.

42 Mike likes to go to his grandmother's school after house.

43 I forgot that had I checked a book out of the library.

44 It is important to look ways both when crossing the street.

45 I planted some seeds in the garden that I'd grown from flowers.

5

Paper 16

Complete the following sentences by selecting the most sensible word from each group of words given in the brackets. Underline the words selected.

Example   The (<u>children</u>, books, foxes) carried the (houses, <u>books</u>, steps) home from the (greengrocer, <u>library</u>, factory).

1 She was very (cross, tired, glad) and said she would like to (stand, sit, run) down.

2 My older (mother, aunt, sister) went to a (school, dance, bag) with her (suitcase, dog, boyfriend).

3 She (left, gave, ate) her (car, pancake, purse) in the (pond, sea, shop).

4 Can you (speak, tell, ring) for the (ambulance, trolley, driving) from your (free, mobile, call) phone?

5 After (breakfast, lunch, supper) the (keys, bikes, moon) came up in the (day, afternoon, sky).

5

Choose the word or phrase that makes each sentence true.

Example   A LIBRARY always has (posters, a carpet, books, DVDs, stairs).

6 A FOREST always has (benches, a lake, paths, flowers, trees).

7 A PIG always has (a name, a tag, a sty, a tail, spots).

8 A HUSBAND is always a (father, man, worker, driver, golfer).

9 A NURSE always works (alone, in a hospital, with patients, at night, in a city).

10 A FLOWER always has (a smell, thorns, roots, two leaves, yellow petals).

5

Underline any word which has the same letter three times.

11 December	Saturday	appears	potato
12 sparrow	trick	eleven	herring
13 individual	indeed	lesson	ironing
14 shines	eatable	release	gossip
15 necessary	alabaster	awkward	series

5

If the code for PLEASED is $+ - \times \div = \times /$, what are the codes for the following words?

16 PLEAD _____ **17** APPLE _____ **18** PALE _____

What do these codes stand for?

19 $/ \div - \times$ _____ **20** $/ \times \times /$ _____

5

Remove one letter from the word in capital letters to leave a new word. The meaning of the new word is given in the clue.

Example   A U N T   an insect   _ant_

21 CREATE   a box   _____

22 SOLID   bought by someone _____

23 WHOLE   an opening   _____

24 HEARD   not soft   _____

25 SUPPER   great   _____

5

Underline the word in the brackets closest in meaning to the word in capitals.

Example   UNHAPPY (unkind   death   laughter   sad   friendly)

26 PUPILS   (teacher   parents   friends   children   neighbours)

27 FELT TIPS   (rulers   writing   books   paper   pens)

28 SOUNDS   (whispers   shouts   silence   noises   cries)

29 HOUSE   (office   shed   bungalow   castle   airport)

30 CHEST   (arm   leg   box   suitcase   crate)

5

Underline the pair of words most opposite in meaning.

Example   cup, mug   coffee, milk   hot, cold

31 beginning, end   unkind, stern   safe, alive

32 smooth, soft   open, closed   first, fast

33 pick, pack   high, low   short, call

34 strong, weak   up, above   eat, food

35 sleep, tired   noise, shout   quiet, loud

5

Find the three-letter word which can be added to the letters in capitals to make a new word. The new word will complete the sentence sensibly.

Example The cat sprang onto the MO. <u>USE</u>

36 My FRIS are all coming to my party. _____

37 Sixty MIES make an hour. _____

38 The building is very new and MRN. _____

39 We moved here three YS ago. _____

40 The police are offering a RED of £1000. _____

5

Underline the word in each line which uses only the first six letters of the alphabet.

41	bake	bread	feed	abbot
42	black	face	dear	bale
43	band	aces	bead	abbey
44	fade	dream	dare	bake
45	deep	beak	bill	add

5

Now go to the Progress Chart to record your score! Total **45**

Paper 17

Here is a weather chart showing hours of sunshine.

Average hours of sunshine per day

	Apr	May	Jun	July	Aug	Sept	Oct
Costa del Sol	8	10	11	11	11	9	7
Costa Brava	8	8	9	10	9	7	5
London	6	7	7	7	6	5	3

1 How many hours of sunshine should the Costa Brava have each day in July? ___

2 The Costa del Sol should get ___ hours of sunshine each day in August.

3 In July the Costa del Sol should have ___ hours of sunshine each day.

4 The Costa Brava should get ___ hours of sunshine each day in April.

5 London should get ___ hours of sunshine each day in October.

5

Underline the pair of words most opposite in meaning.

Example   cup, mug   coffee, milk   <u>hot, cold</u>

6   sand, beach   heavy, light   tired, sleepy

7   run, around   write, ink   here, there

8   better, best   whisper, shout   read, write

9   late, early   fish, meat   cat, dog

10   talk, speak   date, year   glad, sad   **5**

Find the three-letter word which can be added to the letters in capitals to make a new word. The new word will complete the sentence sensibly.

Example   The cat sprang onto the MO.   <u>USE</u>

11   The runners RD each other to win.   _____

12   The PAR is a bird usually kept in a cage.   _____

13   'Do up the BUTS on your shirt!'   _____

14   Tim liked BN sugar on his cereal.   _____

15   Nishpa ENS the festival of Diwali.   _____   **5**

Find the letter which will end the first word and start the second word.

Example   peac (<u>h</u>) ome

16   han (__) eal   17   mat (__) nds   18   sal (__) wo

19   duc (__) now   20   mas (__) rack   **5**

Look at the first group of three words. The word in the middle has been made from the other two words. Complete the second group of three words in the same way, making a new word in the middle.

Example   PAIN   INTO   TOOK   ALSO   <u>SOON</u>   ONLY

21   HOME   MEAN   ANTS   SANE   _____   STAY

22   GREY   EYES   ESPY   EACH   _____   INCH

23   TEST   TEAR   ARTS   BATH   _____   SHED

24   LARK   LINK   SING   BEST   _____   NEAR

25   FIRE   FISH   SHOP   BEAR   _____   STEW   **5**

Underline the two words, one from each group, which are closest in meaning.

Example (race, shop, start) (finish, begin, end)

26 (fire, help, hinder)   (call, after, aid)

27 (ruin, match, result)   (mend, spoil, again)

28 (hate, angry, soft)   (cross, hard, fallen)

29 (talk, chat, hear)   (see, listen, cost)

30 (price, garment, till)   (shop, label, cost)

5

Rearrange the muddled words in capital letters so that each sentence makes sense.

Example   There are sixty SNODCES SECONDS in a UTMINE MINUTE.

31–32 We have a DNBA _____ in our SASLC _____ .

33–34 I like playing the MURDS _____ . Mr Brown plays the AIONP _____ .

35 We make a lot of ONSIE _____ .

5

Underline the number that completes the sentence.

36 6 is to 36 as 7 is to (49, 28, 56)

37 12 is to 9 as 40 is to (12, 20, 30)

38 14 is to 21 as 21 is to (24, 28, 32)

39 4 is to 20 as 50 is to (80, 250, 100)

40 19 is to 38 as 38 is to (19, 76, 50)

5

Underline the word in brackets closest in meaning to the word in capitals.

Example   UNHAPPY   (unkind death laughter sad friendly)

41 PIP   (fruit flower seed skin flesh)

42 FROSTY   (cold snowy icy bright bitter)

43 SKID   (roll trip slide tumble brake)

44 RAISE   (upright tall lift drop collect)

45 LEAN   (tilt bend fat hungry curve)

5

1–5 Look at these groups of words.

Group A Kitchen things   Group B Languages

Group C Birds   Group D Animals

Choose the correct group for each of the words below. Write in the letter.

whisk __   camel __   Dutch __   scales __   gull __

German __   lamb __   recipe __   goose __   French __

5

Find the three-letter word which can be added to the letters in capitals to make a new word. The new word will complete the sentence sensibly.

Example   The cat sprang onto the MO.   <u>USE</u>

6 Have you seen the fish in the WR?   _____

7 He was wearing a stripy SF.   _____

8 You must SH the money with Nina.   _____

9 Put the HING out to dry on the line.   _____

10 No one saw him SL the money.   _____

5

Find the letter which will end the first word and start the second word.

Example   peac (<u>h</u>) ome

11 lan (__) own   **12** fea (__) urn   **13** gon (__) lass

14 sto (__) lace   **15** rop (__) ar

5

Fill in the crosswords so that all the given words are included. You have been given one letter as a clue in each crossword.

16

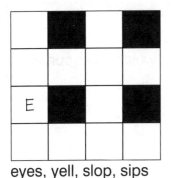

eyes, yell, slop, sips

17

acts, flag, food, oats

2

Change the first word of the third pair in the same way as the other pairs to give a new word.

> **Example** bind, hind   bare, hare   but, <u>hut</u>

18 and, sand   ill, sill   eat, _____

19 bet, best   cot, cost   lit, _____

20 cat, coat   bat, boat   mat, _____

21 fat, feat   mat, meat   hat, _____

22 is, this   at, that   an, _____

5

If the code for VEGETABLE is + / − / × @ $ = /, what are the codes for the following words?

23 GET _____   **24** BLEAT _____   **25** LEAVE _____

What do these codes stand for?

26 × @ − _____   **27** − @ × / _____

5

A and B wear blue jeans. C and B wear red shirts. D and A wear green shirts. C and D wear black jeans.

28 Who wore blue jeans and a red shirt?   —

29 Who wore black jeans and a green shirt?   —

30 Who wore blue jeans and a green shirt?   —

31 Who wore black jeans and a red shirt?   —

4

32 Underline the word which uses only the first six letters of the alphabet.

dear   cedar   bead   feast   aside

1

If the following letters were arranged in alphabetical order, which letter comes in the middle?

33 CRIED   _____

34 BROKE   _____

35 SWEPT   _____

3

Complete the following sentences by selecting the most sensible word from each group of words given in the brackets. Underline the words selected.

Example The (<u>children</u>, books, foxes) carried the (houses, <u>books</u>, steps) home from the (greengrocer, <u>library</u>, factory).

36 I studied my (<u>words</u>, letters, numbers) because we had a (running, art, <u>spelling</u>) test at (home, <u>school</u>, camp).

37 The (painter, butcher, <u>writer</u>) worked alone in her (car, <u>study</u>, desk) trying to finish her (poet, works, <u>book</u>).

38 When the plane (<u>landed</u>, swam, ran) we (waved, broke, <u>dropped</u>) into (silence, <u>applause</u>, cheers).

39 My (<u>sister</u>, brother, father) got a ring from her (cat, <u>boyfriend</u>, baby) for her (lunch, job, <u>birthday</u>).

40 The actress (found, lost, <u>spent</u>) the (second, <u>weekend</u>, years) learning her (<u>lines</u>, characters, costume).

5

Underline the pair of words most similar in meaning.

Example come, go <u>roam, wander</u> fear, fare

41 leave, depart   run, sit   sleep, awake

42 rough, smooth   half, whole   bitter, sour

43 messy, neat   calm, peaceful   rude, polite

44 sweep, brush   loose, tight   hungry, full

45 straight, crooked   grateful, thankful   less, more

5

Now go to the Progress Chart to record your score!   Total   45

Paper 19

Underline the word in brackets closest in meaning to the word in capitals.

Example UNHAPPY   (unkind death laughter <u>sad</u> friendly)

1 SIMILAR   (different wrong same familiar smile)

2 TALK   (shout say whisper argue cry)

3 ALLOW   (stop low ask let all)

4 DEAR   (sweet light honest dare beloved)

5 BEECH   (sand sea tree plant branch)

5

Find the three-letter word which can be added to the letters in capitals to make a new word. The new word will complete the sentence sensibly.

Example   The cat sprang onto the MO. U̲S̲E̲

6 The tennis CTS were fully booked.   _____

7 The police issued a WART for his arrest.   _____

8 My sister wears ARMDS for swimming.   _____

9 When the sun shines I can see my SOW.   _____

10 I need to SHAR my pencil.   _____

5

Find the letter which will end the first word and start the second word.

Example   peac (h̲) ome

11 gat (__) ase

12 min (__) act

13 zon (__) tch

14 ben (__) rim

15 als (__) dds

5

Give the missing letters or numbers in each sequence. The alphabet has been written out to help you.

A B C D E F G H I J K L M N O P Q R S T U V W X Y Z

Example   CQ   DQ   EP   FP   G̲O̲

16 A   D   G   J   ____   P

17 2B   4D   6F   8H   ____   12L

18 ABD   CDF   EFH   GHJ   ____   KLN

19 MAB   NBC   OCD   PDE   ____   RFG

20 9AB   8CD   7EF   6GH   ____   4KL

5

Fill in the crosswords so that all the given words are included. You have been given one letter as a clue in each crossword.

21

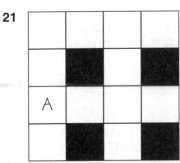

dale, leap, alas, deal

22

pain, into, note, pint

23

slow, site, week, type

3

Rearrange the muddled letters in capitals to make a proper word. The answer will complete the sentence sensibly.

Example A BEZAR is an animal with stripes. _ZEBRA_

24 We came at last to the ALECST gate. _____

25 Has AOEYNN seen my pen? _____

26 The IPREAT had a bag of money and a parrot. _____

27 We're going to the NICEAM tomorrow evening. _____

28 Please can you do the GNIPOPSH today? _____

5

These words have been written in code, but the codes are not under the right words.

TOP	POT	TOO	TON	NOTE
6417	144	146	541	145

Write the correct code for each word.

29 TOP   30 POT   31 TOO   32 TON   33 NOTE

___   ___   ___   ___   ___

5

Complete the following sentences by selecting the most sensible word from each group of words given in the brackets. Underline the words selected.

> **Example** The (<u>children</u>, books, foxes) carried the (houses, <u>books</u>, steps) home from the (greengrocer, <u>library</u>, factory).

34 The (queen, king, prince) who lived in a (shed, train, castle) only wore her (hair, shoes, crown) for special occasions.

35 I set my alarm (pen, torch, clock) for seven o'clock because I wanted to be (on time, late, known) for my first day at (school, moon, tea).

36 During the (summer, winter, autumn) we sometimes get (snow, rain, clouds) which means we get to go (sledging, eating, sun bathing).

37 When I feel (well, ill, happy) my grandmother gives me some (medicine, trousers, glasses) to help me feel (sad, worse, better).

4

Remove one letter from the word in capital letters to leave a new word. The meaning of the new word is given in the clue.

> **Example** A U N T   an insect   <u>ant</u>

38 SNAP   a rest   _____

39 SPEND   to tell to go   _____

40 SPOKE   to push or jab   _____

41 SPOIL   dirt or earth   _____

42 HAUNT   a relative   _____

5

If the word DAUGHTERS is written in code as 123456789, what is the sum of these words?

43 D + A + T + E = _____

44 R + E + A + D = _____

45 T + R + E + E = _____

3

Paper 20

Complete these questions. The alphabet has been given to help you.

A B C D E F G H I J K L M N O P Q R S T U V W X Y Z

Example   AB is to CD as PQ is to RS

1 A35 is to B40 as C45 is to ___

2 29A is to 31B as 33C is to ___

3 AZ is to BY as CX is to ___

4 AB is to CD as EF is to ___

5 W is to V as U is to ___

5

Fill in the missing number in each sequence.

Example   2   4   6   8   10

6   1   2   4   7   ___   16

7   40   36   ___   28   24   20

8   5   10   15   ___   25   30

9   24   21   ___   15   12   9

10 7   14   21   28   ___   42

5

These words have been written in code, but the codes are not under the correct words. One code is missing.

RAN   ADD   RAIN   RING   AND

4751   4275   256   266

Write the correct code for each word.

11 RAN   12 ADD   13 RAIN   14 RING   15 AND

_____   _____   _____   _____   _____

5

If the word MARIGOLD is written in code as 12345678, what is the sum of these words?

16 G + O + L + D = ___   17 G + R + I + M = ___

18 L + A + I + R = ___

3

57

Underline the two words which are made from the same letters.

Example   TAP   PET   <u>TEA</u>   POT   <u>EAT</u>

19 INCH   CHAP   CHIN   NICE   PACK

20 CRUSH SHUSH BRUSH SHRUB BUNCH

21 RAIN   NEAT   NEAR   EARN   TENT

22 CLASP CLASS SCORE PLACE SCALP

○ 4

Change one word so that the sentence makes sense. Underline the word you are taking out and write your new word on the line.

Example   I waited in line to buy a <u>book</u> to see the film.   *ticket*

23 I ran out of toothpaste so couldn't brush my feet.   _____

24 The pig barked to be let into the house.   _____

25 'It isn't my reason that the window is broken!'   _____

○ 3

Underline the pair of words most similar in meaning.

Example   come, go   <u>roam, wander</u>   fear, fare

26 young, old   brief, short   good, bad

27 in, out   better, worse   glad, happy

28 dark, light   yell, scream   colour, plain

29 talk, speak   cold, hot   bed, time

30 read, story   see, look   eat, food

○ 5

Find the three-letter word which can be added to the letters in capitals to make a new word. The new word will complete the sentence sensibly.

Example   The cat sprang onto the MO.   <u>USE</u>

31 We TLED through the crowds.   _____

32 The SPACES landed on the moon.   _____

33 The eagle SED effortlessly.   _____

34 We FOLED the path to the sea.   _____

35 The player SCO a goal.   _____

Find the letter which will end the first word and start the second word.

Example   peac (<u>h</u>) ome

36 hai (_) ean   **37** mos (_) ime

38 pai (_) rip   **39** bel (_) hen

40 cak (_) ven

5

Underline two words, one from each group, that go together to form a new word. The word in the first group always comes first.

Example   (hand, <u>green</u>, for)   (light, <u>house</u>, sure)

41 (birth, help, cradle)   (less, more, much)

42 (pick, slow, set)   (end, back, forward)

43 (in, smoke, match)   (fire, water, stick)

44 (dirty, mess, clean)   (time, old, age)

45 (let, come, in)   (room, doors, stairs)

5

Now go to the Progress Chart to record your score!   Total   45

Progress Chart   Verbal Reasoning 8-9 years

Total marks ▼   Paper ▼

| | 1 | 2 | 3 | 4 | 5 | 6 | 7 | 8 | 9 | 10 | 11 | 12 | 13 | 14 | 15 | 16 | 17 | 18 | 19 | 20 | Percentage ▼ |

45 — 100%
40 — 90%
35 — 80%
30 — 70%
— 60%
25 — 50%
20 — 40%
15 — 30%
10 — 20%
5 — 10%
0 — 0%

| 1 | 2 | 3 | 4 | 5 | 6 | 7 | 8 | 9 | 10 | 11 | 12 | 13 | 14 | 15 | 16 | 17 | 18 | 19 | 20 |

Date ▶

When you've finished the book read the Next Steps ➡